The Diana Phenomenon

Francis Bridger

Vicar of St Mark's Church, Woodthorpe, Nottingham

GROVE BOOKS LIMITED
RIDLEY HALL RD CAMBRIDGE CB3 9HU

Contents

The Cover Illustration is by Peter Ashton

First Impression September 1998
ISSN 0144-171X
ISBN 1 85174 383 9

1
The Puzzle

The week that followed Princess Diana's death on 31 August 1997 revealed a depth of reaction that stunned the world. Nobody had anticipated such a phenomenon and even now it remains difficult to explain. So what lay behind it and what significance does it continue to hold for us? The task of this booklet is to explore these questions.

To make sense of the Diana phenomenon we must first understand that Diana was far more than an individual. She was a potent social and cultural symbol possessing an enormous capacity to arouse loyalty, love and grief on a world-wide scale. She stood for a great deal more than the shallow soap opera of a Royal marriage gone wrong. Diana was, in the profoundest sense, a postmodern icon who resonated with the deepest instincts and feelings of contemporary culture.

The extent to which this is the case has hardly been grasped by the Christian church. Although postmodernism has been the flavour of the month in academic circles for some time, only now is it beginning to seep into public consciousness. Among the majority of Christians, it is hardly recognized let alone discussed. Yet Diana's death and the massive reaction it engendered cry out for interpretation which can only be done by reference to cultural theory—in short, a theory of postmodernity.[1]

But this is not simply a matter of intellectual theorizing, crucial though that may be. The Diana phenomenon throws up important *practical* issues for the church: the gap between what Christians publicly say they believe and what most non-churchgoers actually believe; the cultural willingness to talk of spirituality while rejecting organized religion; the sense of existential angst and despair brought to the surface by Diana's death; the groping after some kind of meta-physical transcendence, as evidenced by the vigils, candles, flowers and tributes in the books of condolence. All these are profoundly *pastoral* issues.

This essay has been written, therefore, in the hope of offering a contribution to a debate which is as much about contemporary society as it is about Diana—a society in the throes of transition from modernity to postmodernity of which Diana was both symbol and victim.

---

1 The literature on postmodernity and postmodernism is vast. For a selection, see Thomas Docherty, *A Reader in Postmodernism* (Brighton: Harvester/Wheatsheaf, 1993); David Lyon, *Postmodernity* (Buckingham: Open University Press, 1994); Zygmunt Bauman, *Intimations of Postmodernity* (London & New York: Routledge, 1992); Bauman, *Postmodernity and Its Discontents* (Cambridge: Polity Press, 1997). For a theological overview, see: Stanley J Grenz, *A Primer on Postmodernism* (Grand Rapids: Eerdmans, 1996); J Richard Middleton & Brian J Walsh, *Truth is Stranger Than It Used To Be* (London: SPCK, 1995). For specifically pastoral issues, see: David Lyall, *Pastoral Care in a Postmodern Context* (Church Westcote: Clinical Theology Association, 1995); Francis Bridger & David Atkinson, *Counselling in Context* (London: DLT, revised edition, 1998), Appendix; Paul Goodliff, *Care in a Confused Climate: Pastoral Care and Postmodern Culture* (London: DLT, 1997).

2
An Icon is Made

At the time of her death, Diana was revered as a postmodern icon even by those who had little understanding of the term.[2] But icons are *made* not *born*. This distinction is crucial for it tells us a great deal both about Diana and about the challenges that postmodernity presents to the church and its ministry.

What was it that turned Diana from a shy aristocratic teenager into an international figure capable of eliciting devotion on an unprecedented scale? At one level, the answer is simple: she married the Prince of Wales. Without her marriage to Charles, Diana would have remained another earl's daughter waiting to be married into the diminishing gene pool that is the British nobility.

But the mere fact of her marriage was not enough to elevate her to iconhood. There had to be more. To be sure, her charm, naïveté, beauty and lack of pretension drew almost everyone under her spell. Even the professional cynic Clive James, although describing her sometimes as 'a fruitcake on the rampage,' confessed himself 'smitten' at first sight.[3]

But this alone could not account for Diana's rise. Nor is it possible to point to any great achievements of the kind usually associated with figures of world renown—she founded no institutes, think-tanks or trusts. She was an indifferent public speaker, had no higher education and wrote nothing very much except thank-you letters.[4] But for all that, she made a greater impact on far more people than politicians who have founded presidential libraries or institutes.

To understand the Diana phenomenon consequently requires something more than superficial explanations. Diana was a cultural symbol who resonated powerfully with those deep forces at work in the transition of Western culture from modernity to postmodernity. This transition began at the start of her life and was in full swing at the time of her death. In her ambiguities and ambivalences, Diana therefore straddled two realities: she was born a modern yet died a postmodern. She truly represented the plight of that postmodern world of which she was ineluctably a part.

1. The Dominance of Image

To most people, Diana was little more than a succession of media images. First the fairytale bride, then the young mother, followed by the tragic wife and finally the caring 'People's Princess.' It has been said that by the time of her death, not a day passed without her face appearing on the cover of a magazine somewhere in

---

2   For an interesting discussion of Diana as icon, see Sir Roy Strong, 'An Icon for the Meritocratic Age' in Brian MacArthur (ed), *Requiem: Memories and Tributes* (London: Pavilion Books, 1997) pp 131-135.
3   Clive James, 'No' in MacArthur, *op cit*, p 84.
4   On Diana's letter-writing see Rosa Monckton's contribution in MacArthur, *op cit*, p 60.

the world. Such was the power of her image that a single intimate photograph could command thousands of pounds. Hence the paparazzi phenomenon that many blamed for her end.

Diana herself was highly ambivalent about the media. She loathed the invasion of her privacy and especially that of her sons. Yet she also recognized the extent of media power. She seemed to possess an intuitive feel for being photographed and from the beginning exercised great charm towards members of the media whom she early came to realize would define her in the eyes of the public.

This has led some to decry her as merely a media manipulator, using every appearance as a performance designed to make people believe her to be something she was not. Certainly, such a reaction was to be heard quite volubly following her infamous *Panorama* interview in 1995 in which she confessed her adultery following the breakdown of her marriage, sought to explain her previous eating disorders in terms drawn from 'pop' psychology and declared her wish to become 'Queen of people's hearts.'

Yet it might reasonably be said in reply that she was doing no more than counter-manipulating those who sought to manipulate *her*. As Clive James put it: 'What else does a marionette dream of except pulling strings?'[5] From her perspective, particularly by the late 1980s, she was confronted by the stark reality of having to face the power of the Establishment alone ('the men in grey suits' as she called them). Faced—as she saw it—by the might of the Royal disinformation machine, she looked on the media as the only opportunity for her to present her point of view. They were the countervailing power to whom she could appeal over and against the forces ranged against her.

This makes for a fascinating human tale. But at a deeper level, it illustrates the force of the postmodernist analysis offered by Baudrillard and others.[6] According to this, 'reality' is not discovered but constructed. It does not exist as something independent of human minds, waiting to be found and reported. Rather, what we call 'reality' is constituted by human beings through the use of language. On this view, everything is a matter of interpretation, nothing is so-called neutral 'fact.' In the words of J Hillis Miller, 'language is not an instrument or tool in man's hands, a submissive means of thinking. Language rather thinks man and his "world."'[7]

As Miller implies, language is a matter of power. For whoever acts as interpreter wields great authority. And since the media not only describe but interpret as well, it follows that they possess enormous power. In the life of Diana we can thus see the twin postmodernist themes of image and power brought together.

There is, however, a further point to be made. In Baudrillard's view, it is not that images *mediate* reality, as the term media implies. Rather, there is *nothing but* images (Baudrillard calls this 'hyperreality'). As David Lyon puts it: 'For

5   *Requiem*, p 88.
6   See David Lyon, *Postmodernity* (Buckingham: Open University Press) pp 15-16, 45-50.
7   quoted in J Richard Middleton & Brian Walsh, *Truth Is Stranger Than It Used To Be* (London: SPCK, 1995) p 51.

Baudrillard, the new electronic media presage a world...of media images that have become the "real," or rather, that erode any distinction between the "real" world and that of the pervasive media.'[8] It is this media world which shapes our view of reality. Or rather, it *constructs* reality for us.[9]

The implications of this are huge. But for our purposes we need simply ask one question: how do we know who Diana truly was? On Baudrillard's view, we *cannot* know. All we can speak of is the person conveyed by media images: the figure constructed by hyperreality. We are confronted by Diana the image and nothing more.

The difficulty with such a view is that it easily leaves us high and dry, suspecting every media image as nothing more than a falsehood employed in some kind of power game. On this basis we would have to live in a state of continual suspicion and disbelief—in effect, a perpetual state of paranoia.

Moreover, when applied to Diana we would be faced with painful questions indeed: was she merely a scheming, cynical manipulator? Were her apparent commitments to good causes genuine? Were the charities she supported just pawns in her power game? Did she *really* care about the AIDS victims and lepers she embraced?

Such an interpretation, however, seems too extreme, if for no other reason than that the many hundreds of people she came to know in person speak with one voice in testifying to her character. Richard Attenborough sums them up: 'She wanted above all to help those who had no voice and were helpless.'[10] From their point of view she was the caring princess, not the cynical manipulator. As far as they were concerned, the media image matched the first-hand reality.

2. The Problem of Identity

In her 17 years of public life, Diana reinvented herself (or was reinvented by others) several times. Her public persona moved through a series of stages: the shy, gauche young girl engaged (and then married) to the most eligible bachelor in the world; the princess learning one day to become queen; the doting mother of the heirs to the throne. These three stages lasted till the late 1980s. A further series of personae followed: the victimized wife; the innocent party trapped in a marriage arranged for the convenience of the House of Windsor; the vessel used for the production of a Royal successor and then dumped. They all add up to the impression of a victim. But by the time of the *Panorama* interview in 1995, she had switched yet again: no longer the victim but instead the New Woman resolutely taking charge of her life; the compassionate heroine, the outsider identifying with the marginalized, and the thwarted romantic all rolled into one.

8   Lyon, p 48.
9   On the idea of reality as socially constructed, see Peter Berger & Thomas Luckmann, *The Social Construction of Reality* (Harmondsworth: Penguin, 1981); Vivien Burr, *An Introduction to Social Constructionism* (London: Routledge, 1995); John R Searle, *The Construction of Social Reality* (London: Penguin, 1996).
10   *Requiem*, p 83.

To say this is not to speak cynically. It is simply to note that whatever else it was, Diana's public identity was highly malleable. To be sure, there were features of her core self which had been constant since childhood: on one hand, her kindness, generosity, lack of pretension and sociability; on the other, her lack of self-esteem, her need for male love and her essential sadness. Both strands persisted throughout her life.

But overlaying them remained the problem of the public self. From 1981 onwards, Diana never felt able fully to 'be herself' (whatever that might have meant) for fear of failing in her duty to the Royal Family. Consequently, like so many public figures, she lived a life comprising many selves—a condition described by Kenneth Gergen as multiphrenia: 'In place of an enduring core of deep and indelible character there is a chorus of invitations.'[11]

It is this plasticity of identity that Zygmunt Bauman sees as the central feature of the postmodern self. Whereas modern (that is to say, Enlightenment) views of the self assumed certain stable, universal characteristics such as autonomy and rationality, postmodernity proposes a self that is pliable, unstable and culturally conditioned. As Bauman puts it: 'The meaning of identity…refers to both persons and things…The world construed of durable objects has been replaced with disposable products designed for immediate obsolescence. In such a world, identities can be adopted and discarded like a change of costume.'[12] Or, to quote Gergen once more, 'If identities are essentially forms of social construction, then one can be anything at any time so long as the roles, costumes and settings have been commodiously arranged.'[13]

As we look back at Diana's life, we can see that in this respect she was authentically postmodern. She made and remade herself as contingencies demanded. Or, more accurately, she remade herself and was *remade* by society and the media. It was a dialectical process. She was above all things a postmodern *product* created in part by herself but even more by the demands of a consumer culture bent on getting the Diana it wanted. Hers was a *socially-constructed* self.

3. The Solitary Self[14]

The postmodern self is a very lonely creation. The autonomous, rational self of modernity carried the burden of loneliness too but, at the same time, felt certain of its essential stability and destiny. By contrast, the pliable self of postmodernity bears the weight of solitariness without any certainty at all. It is condemned to exist as if it could rely only on itself. And since such a self is constantly in flux, it follows that the self on which it is supposed to rely is nothing more than a chimera. To quote Bauman again: '*The hub of postmodern life strategy is*

---

11   Quoted in Middleton & Walsh, *op cit*, p 55.
12   Zygmunt Bauman, *Postmodernity and Its Discontents* (Cambridge: Polity Press, 1997) p 88.
13   Middleton & Walsh, *op cit*, p 53.
14   For a discussion of the postmodern self, see Middleton & Walsh, *op cit*, chapter 3; Charles Taylor, *Sources of the Self: The Making of the Modern Identity* (Princeton: Princeton University Press, 1987); Seyla Benhabib, *Situating the Self* (Cambridge: Polity Press, 1992).

not making identity stand—but the avoidance of being fixed' (his italics).[15]
There is an even more devastating consequence of this fluidity—the impossibility of making durable relationships. Life becomes a series of episodic encoun-
ters, contingent upon the needs and whims of the self at any given moment. Deep,
enduring relationships become difficult to enter into and difficult to sustain.
Middleton and Walsh put it well:

> By definition, a saturated, multiphrenic self will find it problematic to enter
> into a relationship of commitment and authenticity. Such relationships neces-
> sarily assume that there is a real self (a real 'me') that is being known and
> loved. How could a postmodern self ever make such a commitment? Who
> would be the *I* in the *I do*? Is this why we see an incredible difficulty with
> commitment in our culture?[16]

Diana was caught in exactly such a trap. Clive James records his surprise at how
ready she was to reveal her innermost thoughts to strangers at the drop of a hat.
Inviting him to lunch after only a single two-minute meeting some time before,
Diana proceeded to spill her innermost confidences. According to James, 'Her
own marriage, she said, was coming apart. She told me why and how. I could
hardly credit my ears. Armed with nothing else except what she told me then, I
could have gone to a telephone and blown the whole thing sky high.'[17]

Andrew Morton, her biographer and chronicler, makes a similar point. In sup-
plying information for his book, Diana insisted they never meet so that she could
not be identified as having cooperated in the book's production. Consequently,
Morton conducted his interviews by proxy, using a trusted intermediary who
carried a list of questions to the Princess which she would then answer privately
by speaking into a tape recorder. Of the very first interview session, Morton re-
marks that 'I was stunned by Diana's candour and disbelieving of the astonishing story she revealed...although lots of questions had been prepared beforehand,
once the tape recorder was switched on her words spilled out of her, almost without interruption and with her barely pausing for breath.'[18]

It was in the most startling image of her latter years, however, that the dilemma of the solitary self was most starkly illustrated—the picture of the solitary
princess sitting alone at the Taj Mahal. Commentators at the time interpreted it as
a pose designed to symbolize her separation from her husband. In fact, the picture symbolized much more. At that moment, Diana authentically represented
the postmodern self. Without realizing it, she stood for the fundamental dilemma
of the postmodern individual—the utter loneliness of what Christopher Lasch
has termed 'the minimal self' which has only itself to rely on and which must

15 Bauman, *op cit*, p 89.
16 *ibid*, p 57.
17 Brian MacArthur (ed), *Requiem*, p 88.
18 Andrew Morton, *Diana: Her True Story in Her Own Words* (London: Michael O'Mara Books, 1997) p 18.

constantly struggle to maintain an image to itself and to the world. Nothing could more accurately sum up Diana.

4. The Ultimacy of Sensation and Pleasure

In his analysis of postmodern culture, Zygmunt Bauman makes the point that in contemporary Western societies individuals are no longer primarily producers or purveyors of goods, as in the high point of industrialism, but instead are regarded as consumers of sensations. The archetypal person no longer finds his or her identity in making things but in experiencing pleasures. He or she, once in 'the role of *goods-purveyor*...has found him/herself in the position of a *goods-consumer*, lived as the role of a *pleasures-collector*—or, more exactly, a *sensations-gatherer*.'[19]

It is no coincidence that this accurately characterizes the 1980s—the decade in which Diana's public and private personae were being formed and re-formed. Thatcher's Britain moved from being a corporatist collective to becoming a market-oriented, privatized haven for individualism. It was during this period that the shift from goods-production to pleasure-consumption was most decisively marked. And it was in this period also that Diana found herself having to make and remake herself after the (shifting) images of the age.

The rise of the sensation-gatherer was typified, according to Bauman, by a growing obsession with physical fitness. Certainly this was true for Diana whose daily trips to the gym supervised by a personal trainer became the subject of much press attention. But Bauman's point is deeper than merely noting a social fad. He argues convincingly that the elevation of fitness to the status of an overriding life goal became inevitable once sensation-gathering had become *the* cultural paradigm: 'The postmodern body is first and foremost a receiver of *sensations*; it imbibes and digests *experiences*; the capacity of being stimulated renders it an instrument of *pleasure*. That capacity is called fitness...'[20]

But there is a drawback. The demand for sensations and pleasures can never be fulfilled. No sooner is one peak reached than the need to scale another leaps into view. 'The body's capacity for vivid sensation and ecstasy is doomed to be forever short of the elusive ideal...impatience climbs the ceaselessly rising pile of successive disappointments, spurred by suspicion of inadequacy.'[21]

These themes can be seen clearly in Diana's life. Not only did she pursue physical fitness but was also an inveterate sensation-gatherer—the love of fashion, the insistence on personal appearance, the luxury holidays, shopping, even a day out at a theme park with her sons. All were images which illustrate Bauman's thesis. It is perhaps significant that the last public pictures of her life were of Diana the pleasure-collector on holiday with another pleasure-collector, Dodi Fayed. It is also significant that many of those who left condolences after her death referred

19 Zygmunt Bauman, *Life in Fragments* (Oxford: Blackwell, 1995) p 115.
20 Bauman, *op cit*, p 116.
21 *ibid.*

to her having found happiness at last in her pursuit of pleasure with Dodi. In her role as sensation-gatherer, Diana once more symbolized and expressed the spirit of the postmodern age.

But this was not the whole story. Unlike her royal sister-in-law Sarah Ferguson, Diana managed to avoid being identified completely with the conspicuous consumption of the eighties and nineties. Her very public suffering and perceived mistreatment at the hands of the Establishment was almost certainly a factor. But more important was her charity work in which she was able to convey a genuine sense of selflessness. As many testified after her death, she really did care for the marginalized and outcast. Her embrace of AIDS victims at a time when they were regarded as social pariahs, her late-night visits to down-and-outs, her meticulous follow-up of individuals she met while on official charity visits and, at the end, her commitment to the landmine abolition campaign all pointed to something more than sensation-gathering. Diana engaged with the suffering of others for *their* sakes, not merely for hers.

Diana's importance, therefore, lay in much more than her personal qualities. It stemmed from her position as a social symbol whose life resonated with deep-running currents in postmodern culture. It is this which explains her iconic stature not only in life but even more in death.

3

The Tragic Week

The news of Diana's death broke in the early hours of Sunday 31 August 1997. Most Britons, therefore, were not aware of it until they woke to the news several hours later. As the day wore on, it became clear that reaction in Britain and around the world was developing with a momentum nobody had foreseen. It was fast becoming a phenomenon in its own right. To some extent this was because—being a Sunday—there was little other news to distract. But even allowing for this, the speed and depth of reaction were astonishing.

In the week that followed, a generation witnessed events which bore little resemblance to anything they had ever experienced. Even the death of John Kennedy—the nearest comparison in terms of popular reaction—was dwarfed by the national (and international) response to the death of Diana. As the week wore on, the myriad of reactions seemed to coalesce into an unstoppable force which reached deep into the national psyche and every area of national life.

It was an unbelievable seven days. On Sunday, television stations ran incessant reviews of the Princess' life. The documentary genre came into its own as a popular narrative device as opposed to a genre reserved for intellectuals. Hour after hour, the same pictures of Diana's 37 years were recycled time and again until the narrative of her life had become internalized by the millions who watched. By the end of the day we had all become instant Diana historians.

Mid-evening on Sunday, Diana's body was flown back from Paris accompanied by the Prince of Wales and her two sisters. This was televised, setting a pattern for the week. Over the next six days, Diana was the central story in every news bulletin. No aspect of public reaction was left uncovered. By the time of the funeral, Diana's death had become a worldwide *media* phenomenon. As Douglas Davies has remarked, 'Through the televising of events, millions were involved in what is probably the most extensive act of the globalization of death yet witnessed in the world.'[22]

Although public reactions were evident even within the first hours, their intensity caught everyone by surprise. Flowers quickly began to appear in public places, notably at the gates of Kensington Palace (Diana's home), Althorp (the Spencer family seat in Northamptonshire) and Buckingham Palace. By Sunday lunchtime, it was estimated that over 1000 bouquets had been placed at Kensington alone. Crowds of mourners also appeared, many distressed, not knowing how to express or deal with their grief. As time passed, grieving rituals developed—the ever-growing sea of flowers, the photos of Diana and poems written about her left at sites of mourning, candlelit vigils, even alleged visions of the Princess. All these sought to articulate social and individual grief.

The ensuing 24 hours also saw another development: tributes from world figures. Tony Blair's emotional interview outside his local church on Sunday morning (when he declared Diana 'the People's Princess') was followed, among others, by statements from Bill Clinton, Boris Yeltsin, Nelson Mandela and Mother Teresa (herself to die within days). The non-political Diana who never pretended to understand the intricacies of international politics, was being fêted by its foremost representatives—another sign that this was more than just another death of a well-known personality.

Owning Her Death

The week moved on. And as it did so, there surfaced an issue which steadily came to dominate the public mind. It could be expressed in a single word: *ownership*. It was a theme that was to underlie every aspect of the period between the death and the funeral—and beyond. Even now it serves as a *motif* by which we can interpret the death-of-Diana phenomenon.

In most cases, the 'ownership' of a death and the events which follow it rests in the hands of the immediate next-of-kin. It is recognized that families have a right to privacy and to order their affairs as they see fit. After the death of Diana, no such convention prevailed. From the moment it was announced, everything

22 Douglas Davies, *The Death of Princess Diana* (private paper delivered at a research seminar at Durham University on January 10th 1998) p 1. I am grateful to various participants in this seminar for thoughts and discussions which have stimulated my thinking.

became public property in the psychological sense if not the legal. It was assumed that the Princess belonged to the nation in death as much as in life. This was to be perhaps the most defining and striking feature of the week.

The ownership question undoubtedly had its positive side. But it also had its negative: the Royal Family were never given permission to grieve or to shape events as they might have wished. On the contrary, criticism set in from the first day when Diana's sons were taken to church at Balmoral as if nothing had happened. No reference was made to their mother's death in the service and, according to some accounts, the minister continued with his sermon unchanged, even to the extent of including jokes from the Scottish comedian Billy Connolly.

This was but one factor in a growing public unrest. Strong feelings began to be expressed about the geographical isolation of the Royal Family in Scotland, their seeming inability to show emotion, the lack of any tribute to Diana and their perceived failure of leadership. A constant theme was the absence of the Family from London. As a headline in the *Sun* newspaper complained: '*Where is the Queen when the country needs her?* She is 550 miles from London, the focal point of the nation's grief...Every hour [Buckingham] Palace remains empty adds to the public anger at what they perceive to be a snub to the People's Princess.'[23]

At one level, it is possible to see in this the public and collective outworking of the anger normally associated with the grieving process. But at another, it is illustrative of the problem of ownership. For Diana was a figure with whom the public identified closely. In many ways, she was a projection of their own hopes and fears. In anthropological language, she acted as a condensed symbol who embodied the nation's identity in the mid-1990s. Added to this was the fact that she was no longer a Royal, having been stripped of membership of the Family following her divorce. The ownership question thus became doubly problematic: she no longer belonged to the Royal Family, so to whom did she belong? By dubbing her 'the People's Princess,' the Prime Minister had seemed to answer the question. And since the Queen was the People's Sovereign, her duty (it was argued) was to be physically present with the People in London, the city that mattered because it was the capital and because Diana lay in rest there.

Managing the Grief

But at the same time there *was* a family that could rightly lay claim to Diana: the Spencers. As the funeral service in Westminster Abbey showed, however, relations between the Windsors and the Spencers were by no means straightforward. Diana's younger brother Charles, head of the family since the death of his father in 1992, resented the treatment his sister had received at the hands of the Royal Establishment. The week between her death and the funeral consequently involved complex negotiations between the two families through intermediaries. And all the while, the pressure for the Establishment to acknowledge that in some sense the People owned Diana (and thus had a right to influence the funeral ar-

---

23 Quoted in Brian MacArthur, *Requiem*, pp 43–4.

rangements) grew in volume and intensity. The process of grieving, far from being a matter for the families alone, took on multiple dimensions which no doubt made the management of grief by the Windsors especially complicated. In the words of David Runcorn, 'The Royal Family were denied the freedom and right to mourn in their own way.'[24]

In the end, the People won. The Royal Family bowed to public pressure and returned a day early from Balmoral to mix with the crowds outside Buckingham Palace from which the Queen gave a national broadcast on the evening before the funeral. In this she paid tribute to the Princess as 'an exceptional and gifted human being' and made clear she shared the public's 'determination to cherish her memory.'[25] It was enough. Criticism of the Royals soon died away; though it was buried rather than dissolved.

The question of ownership surfaced in other ways. The day after Diana's body was flown home, it was announced that condolence books would be opened in St James' Palace (where Diana lay) for visitors to record their entries. At first, it was thought that five would suffice but it quickly became obvious that these would be hopelessly inadequate for the millions who wished to record their tributes. Within days, no self-respecting town or borough was without its book of condolence, so that by the end of the week it seemed as if the entire nation had written something about Diana. Likewise, British embassies abroad recorded large numbers of people arriving to sign condolence books originally thought necessary for only a few. And on the Internet could be found scores of websites offering the chance to enter comments into electronic books. Of these the official Buckingham Palace site and the BBC site were probably the most visited.

The condolence book phenomenon can be interpreted in several ways. In the first place, it was another instance of the demand for public ownership of Diana and the right to grieve for her. Douglas Davies' comment about the globalization of this particular death through the electronic media is apposite. The opening up of conventional and Internet condolence books represented the globalization of *grief*—a phenomenon impossible even only 10 years earlier but now made possible by the spread of information technology. In death as in life, Diana was proving herself to be a truly postmodern woman.

But the condolence books also represented something else: the victory of what might be called 'democratic consumerism.' Like the demand of the crowds for the Royal Family to return to London, the demand by large numbers of ordinary people to record their grief in the books articulated *en masse* the view that Diana belonged to the People as much as to her 'blood family' (to use her brother's phrase) or the Royal Family. Diana, in so many ways the creation of consumer culture, was thereby reclaimed by that culture as its own. The democratic impulse had triumphed over the quasi-feudal hierarchicalism of the Royal Establishment and 'the system.' Postmodernity had arrived on the back of tragedy.

24 David Runcorn, *Surprised by Grief* (private paper, September 1997) p 10.
25 Quoted in *Requiem*, p 51.

4

Theories Many

In previous chapters we have seen how Diana's death, public reaction to it and the events which surrounded it can be interpreted with the aid of postmodern cultural theory. By itself, however, this is inadequate. The death of Diana phenomenon had many facets, and in order to understand it adequately we must draw upon a range of disciplines. In this chapter and the next, therefore, we shall consider a number of insights drawn from the perspectives of sociology, psychology and theology. This is crucial if we are to take the Diana phenomenon as a paradigm for understanding the challenges and tasks of ministry in the postmodern world.

1. Sociology

Why did such huge numbers of people react to Diana's death in the way they did? The answers to this question are important because they provide significant clues as to the social context in which the church's ministry takes place. The sociologist Tony Walter has suggested three possibilities:[26]

- *'A revival of the Wenceslas notion of monarchy.'* By this Walter means the reawakening of a long-buried belief that royal figures act as mediators between the sacred and the everyday world. He is sceptical of such an interpretation of Diana on the grounds that people no longer have a sense of the sacred and therefore no need for a Wenceslas monarch: 'Why do people particularly want this now?'

  Over and against Walter, however, it could be argued that the nature of postmodern spirituality makes it much more likely that the Wenceslas argument contains an element of truth. As we shall see in chapter five, although postmodern culture has little room for organized religion, it actively encourages the search for the spiritual. In fact, the vaguer and more mystical the better. It is quite possible, therefore, that at the level of unconscious symbol, Diana tapped into the Wenceslas notion and played it out in her everyday life. It is an interpretation worth considering.
- *Diana's personal acts of charity.* Why did people respond so positively towards these? The most obvious answer is that people identified with her compassion and warmth and that it was these qualities that evoked such a response after her death. There is, however, another interpretation offered by such com-

---

26 Tony Walter, 'The Queen of Hearts: A Sociological Reflection' (paper given at a seminar in London on 7 February 1998 at the City Temple, Holborn and subsequently published in *The Church of England Newspaper* 20 February 1998) p 6. Quotations and references are taken from the full text of the paper.

mentators as Ross McKibbin.[27] Observing that the greatest response happened in countries such as the USA and Britain where social solidarity was at its weakest after two decades of market-oriented philosophy, McKibbin concludes that Diana symbolized (and thus legitimated) the substitution of private compassion for social welfare. Walter summarizes McKibbin thus: 'Such countries value personal acts of charity rather than the welfare state, hence they warmed to Di.'

This is a plausible explanation. Two decades of extolling the virtues of the market and the vices of the state no doubt had some effect upon the national consciousness. But even Mrs Thatcher found it impossible to reform the welfare system, let alone dismantle it. And every test of public opinion has consistently suggested that there continues to be widespread support for collective social provision over and against reliance on 'personal acts of charity.' If nothing else, the election of a Labour government in May 1997 demonstrated this. If McKibbin's thesis carries any force at all, it can only be in a severely qualified form.

- *Diana embodied human values not symbolized by national leaders since 1979.* This is Walter's favoured explanation. It is also politically-charged. It effectively argues that Diana filled a gap left by British and American politicians which no other national figure or institution was able to fill, although some, such as the church, had tried with partial success (as, for example, with *Faith in the City*): 'Thatcher seemed to lack compassion, the Windsors seemed unfeeling—thus for twenty years, Britain has lacked leaders who embodied such virtues.'

Walter goes on to develop a much larger sociopolitical argument: 'An industrial society driven by rationality needs powerful figures to articulate basic human virtues: emotionality to balance rationality, care to balance profit, vulnerability to balance efficiency.' Only in the late 1980s did such a figure appear on the scene—Diana 'the wounded healer, the glamorous princess who touched lepers and people with AIDS yet who was herself vulnerable...She embodied all the values denied by economic rationality and political calculation.'

This is a powerful and appealing thesis. But it could go further by taking a gender perspective. If, as Walter contends, the rationalistic 'iron cage' of modernity (to use Max Weber's telling phrase) has so repressed the affective side of society, it is possible to argue that Diana in her person and acting as a social symbol, provided a means by which gentler, kinder virtues traditionally associated with women could find expression in national life. In the words of Bryan Jobbins, 'Diana is the embodiment of the feminine...She represents the emergence of the female principle that is within all of us but has been so long suppressed or marginalized.'[28]

This opens up an interesting train of thought. Politically, Mrs Thatcher was

---

27 Cited in Walter, *ibid.*
28 Bryan Jobbins, 'Diana: a postscript' in *Counselling* (February 1998) p 15.

perceived as being more masculine than most men. She offered a style of leadership which broke decisively with female stereotypes in that its hallmarks were aggression and hardness—typically *masculine* traits. Moreover she did things which only men had done before. She sent armies off to war in the Falklands, celebrated their victory with a military parade, took on the male-dominated trades unions, defeated the miners in 1985 and generally wiped the floor of the House of Commons with her male opponents within and outside her own party. Throughout the 1980s, therefore, there existed a lacuna at the top of British politics—the Prime Minister was a woman who revelled in acting like a man. Other parties were led by men who simply sought to keep up by trying to *imitate* Thatcher. The name of the game was who could be most *macho*.[29] No woman could be found who successfully embodied the traditionally feminine virtues in public life—that is, until Diana.

If Diana filled a gender gap in the national psyche, though, it was precisely because she was *not* a politician. She did not need to out-Thatcher Thatcher. If she *had* been a politician, it is doubtful whether she would had gained the support she did. Her political naïveté was essential to her success. It was crucial that Diana remained a political virgin. It placed her above the fray and left her unsullied in the public mind by the 'grubbiness' of politics. Her political *un*involvement was the guarantee of public trust.

It was no coincidence, therefore, that the virtues Walter identifies as missing in British public life throughout the 1980s (and carried over in only a slightly diluted form in the 1990s) were traditionally *feminine* virtues. Put another way, Diana was the *alter ego* Mrs Thatcher could never assume but which the public wanted.

If there is force in any of the three possibilities put forward by Walter, the church must listen carefully. For taken together they point to a culture which has moved beyond the simplistic, humanist self-confidence of the 1960s and '70s into a period of transition marked by a new search for some kind of transcendence. Postmodernity hardly knows what transcendence means but it *feels* it is out there somewhere and wants to discover it. New Age philosophies notwithstanding, there could scarcely be a more opportune moment for the church.

2. Psychology

From a psychological point of view, Diana's death produced some strange and unexpected results. The Samaritans reported a 6% drop in calls to their national helpline between 31 August and 7 September—exactly the time it might be supposed that stress factors would have produced the opposite. The Samaritans' explanation was simple: 'People are brought closer together by such tragic and significant events, and in this mood of mutual understanding feel more able to talk openly about their inner thoughts and emotions, even sharing them quite

---

29 See Hugo Young, *One of Us: A Biography of Margaret Thatcher* (London: Pan Books, 1990).

intimately with sympathetic strangers.'[30]

If indeed this was the case, it is further evidence in support of the postmodernist contention that individuals in contemporary society suffer from a combination of alienation and solitariness—a lack of community we might call hyper-individualism. Diana's death, by catapulting people into a shared experience of grief, provided a way both of sharing the problem and experiencing a common cathartic response. In Tony Walter's words, 'Mourning can bring people together and when millions mourn together the effect is to demonstrate social solidarity in an almost unparalleled way. Thus, the society that Margaret Thatcher had announced did not exist was symbolically reconstituted in the parks of London and in the cyberspace of electronic condolence.'[31] It is ironic that the deconstruction of community wrought in Diana's lifetime should be reconstructed at her death as a community of *grief*.

Across the Atlantic, other things were happening. David Runcorn tells of the New York therapist who later wrote of her women clients finding themselves 'stunned by the power of their reaction to her death, unable to talk about anything else, obsessed with reading every word and watching every newscast, and dismayed that the men in their lives hadn't a clue what so moved them.'[32] Runcorn interprets this in two ways. Firstly, he draws upon the notion of the 'Significant Other,' the person 'not physically present' in the counselling room 'and often not even consciously recognized for who they are in the client's life. Yet their influence has been/is profound (for good or ill) in shaping the person's self-understanding and response to life.'[33] Diana, he argues, acted as a 'Significant Other' for millions of women worldwide. Hence the international grief when she could no longer fulfil that role. Secondly, he links this to the idea of projection. In a vivid (though possibly unintentional) pun he fuses the counselling use of the term with the popular one: 'Diana had become a blank screen for many people onto whom they could project their own hopes and longings and identify their own struggles.'[34] We might add that if the analysis contained above in chapter two is valid, she did so precisely because she was a postmodern woman calling to other postmodern women.

The Kleinian psychotherapist Bryan Jobbins takes up the significance of Diana's appeal to women, giving it a significant twist. Acknowledging that she was 'the admired role model for a majority of women'[35] he goes on to argue that the phenomenon had its darker side: 'Concealed beneath this imitative admiration was its opposite—envy.' This is an interesting interpretation which Jobbins develops in terms of a tension between Diana's lifestyle (to which many women will have aspired) and the impossibility of achieving it—which will have led some into

---

30 Samaritans' *Newsletter* (undated) p 2.
31 Tony Walter, *ibid.*
32 Runcorn, *Paper*, p 4.
33 *ibid*, p 3.
34 *ibid*, p 4.
35 Bryan Jobbins, 'Diana: a postscript' in *Counselling* (February 1998) p 14.

envy: 'For many women Diana's dazzle was almost blinding. Her life-style was a constant rebuke.' In consequence, when she died, the envy turned into guilt 'for having triumphed over Diana by living.' In Jobbins' view, it is this above all which provides the key to understanding the mass remorse: we all felt guilty at having envied Diana her lifestyle but even more so at having out-lived her. 'We can only begin to make sense of the public's collective guilt and remorse in terms of unacknowledged envy.'

At first sight, this may seem too simplistic. But even if Jobbins is only half correct, a massive question remains unanswered: how has this guilt/envy been dealt with? How has it been worked through at the societal level? Jobbins suggests that the veneration of Diana which set in almost immediately after her death represents one way: 'Idealization replaces envy. It is entirely expiatory.' To this we might add another possibility: that guilt/envy may end up being ritualized in the same way Remembrance Sunday offered (and still offers) a ritual escape from the guilt of remaining alive after the carnage of war. Indeed, there have been suggestions that Diana's death be marked annually by a day of remembrance. But even if such calls for a 'Diana day' are forgotten, it is likely that pilgrimages to Althorp will fulfil a ritual function for those seeking absolution. To view the burial place of the dead princess and to see the relics of her life in the newly-constructed Diana museum may become a postmodern religious act without its participants knowing. Dealing with grief in a postmodern society thus becomes quite different from dealing with it in modernity. The public acknowledgment of feelings and the externalization of grief constitute a step far removed from the controlled repression of the modern period.[36] This is not without implications for the church.

One further point in Jobbins' analysis is worth mentioning. Diana lived a short life, alternately hopeful and sad. In very many ways she represented the essence of postmodern existence—tenuous, episodic, lonely, and fraught with emotionally inadequate and unsatisfying relationships. In so many ways (particularly for women who had trodden the same path as her) Diana's life symbolized our own. Hence the enormous sense of identification with her after death. As Jobbins notes, 'Diana's short life, her sudden death, are facts that represent...our age of fragility and potential fragmentation of our hopes, possibilities.'[37] But it was perhaps in the arena of human emotions that this representation-identification process was strongest. For Diana in public played out the script most of us keep hidden away inside the realm of the private. Her insecurity, her roller-coaster emotional life, misfortunes, loves and hates were public reflections of our own similar feelings. She became the symbol of millions of individual lives. There was 'a mutual sharing with Diana of her emotional vacuum.' In some way, *her* death was therefore *our* death. In grieving for her, we were grieving for ourselves.

---

36 See Tony Walter, *Funerals And How To Improve Them* (London: Hodder & Stoughton, 1990) chapter 2, especially pp 26-8.
37 Jobbins, *ibid*, p 15.

5
And So To Theology...

Theological reflection upon the death of Diana has been slight—or, rather, the amount published has been slight. As time goes by, this will no doubt change. In this chapter we shall attempt to carry discussion forward by considering three themes which deserve attention: Diana's spirituality; Diana and folk religion; and Diana the redemptrix.

Diana's Spirituality

About one thing commentators are agreed: Diana was not conventionally religious. Neither did she adhere to any single body of belief. Rather, her views and practices were eclectic, pragmatic and feelings-led. In short, she was typically postmodern.[38]

The primary evidence for this comes from Diana herself. In the transcripts of her tape-recorded interviews given to Andrew Morton in 1991-92, she speaks of the 'spiritual people' who came into her life 'after I finished my bulimia.'[39] Significantly, the list includes her astrologer and clairvoyant but no churchpeople. Of course, this may simply reflect the fact that the church had been a part of the Royal routine which she dutifully fulfilled but which played no part in her life once she had ceased to be counted as a member of the Royal Family. George Carey expressed the point tactfully in a tribute shortly after her death: 'She had faith in God, although she wasn't the kind of person who wore religion on her sleeves. There was a deep faith there...She didn't associate with institutional Christianity. There was faith in her whole personality.'[40]

But faith in what? The Morton tapes are again revealing. They point to a mishmash of ideas culled from a variety of sources. Diana believed, for example, in *déja vu* ('Places I think I've been before, people I've met') and was convinced that her paternal grandmother Countess Spencer 'looks after me in the spirit world. I know that for a fact.'[41] Moreover, she regularly attempted to contact her through a clairvoyant, claiming that she had actually spoken with the Countess and with other dead people she had known: 'My grandmother came in first, very strong, then my uncle and then Barry [her former police protection officer who had died].' Alongside visits to the clairvoyant went trips to the astrologer Debbie Frank.

---

38 On postmodern spirituality, see articles in *The Way* 36/3 (July 1996). Also, David Hilborn, 'Postmodern Spirituality and the Gospel: Some Pointers from the Death of Diana' (paper given at a seminar in London on 7 February 1998 at the City Temple, Holborn and subsequently published in *The Church of England Newspaper* 20 February 1998) p 6. Quotations refer to the full text of the paper.
39 Andrew Morton, *Diana: Her True Story—In Her Own Words* (London: Michael O'Mara Books, 1997) p 65.
40 Quoted in Brian MacArthur (ed), *Requiem*, p 19.
41 Morton, *op cit*, pp 65–6. This is the location for all quotations from Diana in this section.

These took place regularly, over a period of three years. In a revealing sentence, Diana speaks of Frank's eclectic work: 'She's very sweet. She does astrology and counselling. She doesn't advise, she tells me from her angle...' Nothing could better sum up the pick-and-mix world of New Age spirituality into which Diana entered in her later years.

It should be noted, however, that something of the modernist sceptic still remained, at least about astrology: 'With astrology,' commented Diana, 'I listen to it but don't believe it totally. It's a direction and a suggestion rather than it's definitely going to happen.' And she was sufficiently aware of the scepticism of others to keep quiet about her dalliance with spirits: 'I'd never discuss it with anyone, they would all think I was a nut. I used the word "psychic" to my policemen a couple of times and they have freaked out.'

So why did she dabble? Cosina Somerset, writing in the *Daily Telegraph*, put forward as convincing an explanation as any: 'Diana did not believe conventionally in God but she and I both sought an explanation for life's endless chaos, pain and drama. The point of seeing psychics is that one has a sense that life is predestined.'[42]

What this suggests is that like many of her class and generation, Diana held no fixed views about the religion in which she had nominally been brought up. What's more, she was disinclined to investigate it. Religion, as she saw it, posed no obstacles to dabbling in the occult. Like many of her postmodern contemporaries, she was happy to use the externals of Christianity in the service of her pick-and-mix spirituality.

Diana's Roman Catholic friend Rosa Monckton records two instances which illustrate this. The first took place during a trip to Greece. According to Monckton, 'Diana was not religious in any conventional sense, but she did have a highly-developed spiritual side. On Sunday 17 August, we had docked on the Greek mainland in a small village called Kipazissi, and we went together to the Greek Orthodox Church. While we were there we lit candles for our children, and when we left the church she turned to me and said: "Oh Rosa, I do so love my boys."'[43]

The second occurred during a visit by Monckton to Kensington Palace where 'on her desk...she had a statue of Christ which was draped with rosaries given to her by the Pope and Mother Teresa. When I was there recently, I saw a note in her own hand which read: "You can't comfort the afflicted without afflicting the comfortable."'

What are we to make of all this? In her spirituality, as in so much else, Diana was the paradigm of postmodernity. She groped after transcendence but was unsure what it was. She cobbled together a ragbag of beliefs without a second thought for their coherence or compatibility. What impelled her were feelings ('Oh, Rosa I do so love my boys'), the paramount of which was the need to receive and give love.

---

42 Quoted in MacArthur, p 77.
43 MacArthur, p 64.

We shall return to the theme of love briefly when we consider Diana the redemptrix. But for the moment it is worth noting that it was in her *practice* of love that Diana's postmodern religious outlook came closest to orthodox Christianity. Irrespective of her eclectic beliefs drawn from hither and thither, her evident concern for the vulnerable and marginalized (especially children), expressed in her willingness to identify with and embrace those whom society rejected, provided a more profound definition of *agape* than any sermon or lecture. In a postmodern age, the image of Diana cuddling AIDS victims constituted an eloquent and powerful theological statement.

Diana and Folk Religion

The death of Diana evoked an immense outpouring of emotion. But in doing so, it gave rise to far greater expressions of religious sentiment than might have been expected in a supposedly secular age. Two aspects of the week following her death exemplified this—the condolence books and the funeral service.

The Condolence Books

As yet, no analysis of the condolence books from Britain and overseas has been carried out. Such scholarly endeavour lies in the future. What *is* currently possible, though, is an analysis of the electronic collections of condolences available in cyberspace. In this section we shall consider the entries made on the BBC Diana Website.[44]

The messages contain a mixture of grief, anger, sadness, piety and thanksgiving for Diana's life—in short all the emotions usually associated with the death of a loved one. This is the first point of significance. Without exception, those who entered a message spoke of Diana *as if she were an intimate member of the family*. She was not a distant Royal personage or public figure but instead was the sister, aunt, friend, confidante. The foremost characteristic which strikes the reader, therefore, is the sheer intimacy of the messages. Yet most—if not all—of the correspondents had never even met or seen the Princess in person. All they knew was the media image.

Here, for example, is a typical entry, from Armin of Stuttgart: 'Dear Diana, I didn't know you face to face but I know that you are in my heart and will be for ever.' Likewise, Debbie Lancaster from California wrote: 'I feel a sense of loss yet I never met Diana.' From Samer in Lebanon came the following: 'Dear Princess, we miss you already here in Lebanon. Even if you've never visited us, you've always been in our hearts. When you left us, it was like a mother we lost.' Mary Ward from Harrisburg Pennsylvania began her message with the words, 'I never had a chance to meet the Princess, but...' And from an anonymous writer:

'She is an immense loss to the world as a whole, but more important and revealing is the feeling of so very many people that they have lost a personal

---

44 www.bbc.co.uk/politics97/diana/links.html

friend. It is the mark of a truly remarkable and unique person that she could engender such emotions in so many others, many of whom, like myself, had never even met her.'

The evidence could hardly be clearer: the grief felt by so many throughout the world was *grief for the loss of a loved one*.

This sense of personal loss led to a phenomenon well-known to those who regularly conduct funerals and prepare families for them: *the need to locate the loved one in a benign place such as heaven or peaceful afterlife*. The following selection is representative of such comments:

- 'Diana...May you have a very special place in Heaven with Mother Teresa and Jesus!!'
- 'Dear lady, you can rest in peace...today you are in the most excellent company of our Lord and Mother Theresa.'
- 'Dear Diana...I hope that I will meet you in heaven.'
- 'Dearest Diana...Thank you Red Rose of England and farewell. May God rest her soul in peace.'
- 'Dear Princess...When you left us, it was like a mother we lost. I hope you'll take care of all the people next to you up there.'
- '[Diana] I am sure you will continue to care for humanity from the peaceful place you and Dodi are [sic] now. Rest in peace sweet Princess. We love you.'
- 'Diana...We grieve your loss with distant tears and wish your soul peace.'
- 'Farewell Diana, you are in peace now.'
- 'Diana...Peace at last, may God rest your soul.'
- 'Princess Diana's arrival in heaven is another beautiful jewel in the crown of God. The Angels of Heaven rejoice as a child of God returns home...May God rest her soul.'
- 'I pray with all my heart that she's happy in heaven...'
- 'A bright new star twinkles in the heavens, we will miss all the things you were to us.'
- 'As she looks down...I hope she knows how much we will be reduced by the loss of such a radiant angel who was still only beginning to learn to fly.'
- 'Even though she has passed away...her soul will be rewarded in heaven where she will enjoy the privacy which she hardly had during her life on earth.'

How are we to interpret such comments? At one level, they can be seen as a therapeutic release in which the writers' anger, fears and loss are externalized and engaged with by the use of such metaphysical ideas as heaven, afterlife and eternal peace. The ideas act as a way of making sense of Diana's death and ameliorating the pain. At another level, however, they reveal a truly eclectic collection of beliefs about death which contain traces of largely sub-Christian notions but little more. What is most striking is that *they reveal absolutely no evidence of Christian belief in resurrection* as a regulative concept for interpreting death. It is as if 2000 years of Christian teaching has left no imprint at all on the popular psyche. Christian ministers will recognize the phenomenon well. Modern funerals are essentially memorial services with a bit of religious language thrown in. The entries in the condolence books confirm that we live in a post-Christian culture which retains some of the language and thought-forms of Christianity but severs them from their theological roots. The implications of this for mission and ministry are enormous.

The Funeral

The funeral of Princess Diana was remarkable in a number of ways. First, it was viewed on television by an estimated 2 billion people worldwide, making it 'probably the most extensive act of the globalization of death yet witnessed in the world.'[45] Second, although Anglican in form, the service in fact amounted to a hotchpotch of ingredients held together not by any religious sentiment or beliefs but by a combination of Earl Spencer's speech and Elton John's song. Neither of these contained any theology or identifiable Christian belief; but there is no doubt that they expressed the popular mood. It is significant that the Earl's tribute-cum-polemic literally drew applause from the crowds outside Westminster Abbey and in the Royal Parks of London as they watched the service on giant video screens erected for the purpose.

Thirdly, the service was notable as much for what it omitted as for what it included. It contained, for example, no sermon or homily. The reading by Tony Blair of 1 Corinthians 13 stood alone as ministry of the word. There was no attempt to offer a Christian interpretation of death (or life for that matter). The proclamation of the resurrection was entirely absent, except for the Scripture sentences accompanying the entry of the coffin, which were sung and therefore probably not comprehended by the majority of spectators. And since the power of the sentences resides in their stark and dramatic proclamation as the coffin enters the church, their effect was duly lost.

In fact, it could be argued that the two most striking contributions—Earl Spencer's speech and Elton John's *Candle in the Wind*—although immensely moving, pointed away from Christian faith rather than towards it. What the crowds applauded most in the speech was its lambasting of the tabloid press ('at the opposite end of the moral spectrum' from Diana) and the Royal Family. This was done in tones authentically human but hardly Christian. Similarly, Elton John's reworking of a song originally written with Marilyn Monroe in mind touched people's emotions but said nothing of any religious value.

Finally, there was the odd spectacle of Earl Spencer's addressing Diana in the second person singular as if she were somehow present. 'Today is the chance to say thank you for the way you brightened our lives...We have all despaired at our loss over the past week and only the strength of the message you gave us...has

45 Douglas Davies, *The Death of Princess Diana* (private paper delivered at a research seminar at Durham University on January 10th 1998) p 1.

afforded us the strength to move forward.' And, perhaps most pointedly, 'on behalf of your mother and sisters, I pledge that we, your blood family, will do all we can to continue the imaginative and loving way you were steering these two exceptional young men [her sons] so that their souls are not simply immersed by duty and tradition but can sing openly as you planned.'[46]

There are various ways of interpreting this. On one hand, it might be said that Spencer was simply pouring out his heart and that addressing Diana directly provided a convenient device for doing so. Alternatively, it may be that he was consciously or unconsciously following the example set by Cardinal Hume at a Requiem Mass held in Westminster Cathedral, where the whole of the Cardinal's sermon was addressed directly to Diana.[47]

Whichever of these explanations is true (or neither of them), there remains an interesting theological question: did the Earl believe that Diana was somehow still there in spirit as well as body? If so, did this signal an end to Protestant attitudes to the dead? Whatever the answer, it seems clear that Diana's funeral, like many others in contemporary society, was essentially postmodern in its ambiance while retaining a traditional shell. In the words of Clive Aslet, writing (of all places) in the magazine *Country Life*, 'Part of Diana's appeal in what is regarded as a post-Christian age may have been her apparent openness to the alternative spirituality represented by mediums and astrologers. But Saturday [the funeral] showed that a church service is still the means by which great hurts of national life can be healed.'[48]

In death as in life, Diana epitomized the postmodernity of which she was both icon and paradigm.

Diana the Redemptrix

We have already seen from the comments entered into the BBC Website condolence book that Diana was compared with Mother Theresa. Just as important is the way in which Diana's life and death might be construed as a parable of redemption.

Central to this are the twin concepts of incarnation and *kenosis*. Although highborn, Diana refused to cling to her aristocratic status, preferring instead to 'descend' into ordinary life once she became an adult. By taking jobs as a kindergarten teacher, nanny and cleaner, she eschewed the aristocratic ethos and entered the 'real' world of work in a way not known by any member of the family into which she was to marry.[49] This at once gave her a sense of identification with the general public so that, despite her origins, the billions who grieved her death could say 'she was one of us.' The themes of incarnation and *kenosis* were thus bound together in a uniquely powerful way.

There were other echoes of incarnational theology too. Diana's evident con-

---

46 Quoted in MacArthur. *Requiem*, pp 179–181.
47 For the full text, see MacArthur, pp 46–8.
48 Quoted in MacArthur, p 161.
49 Diana actually enjoyed this ordinary life. See Morton, *op cit*, p 31.

cern for the poor and the vulnerable, her desire to bring healing to the broken lives of others, the sense in which she was able to do so because she herself was a wounded healer were all parables of redemption.[50] Likewise, it could be argued (as did her brother) that she was hounded by her enemies and metaphorically crucified by the Establishment ('the men in grey suits'). Yet she also saw a form of resurrection in her life as she remade herself in the latter years. It is as if her life parabolically embodied the redemptive sequence of descent, identification, crucifixion and resurrection that lies at the heart of New Testament theology.[51]

Too much should not be read into this. However, it is worth noting that for many, Diana could best be characterized by religious comparisons. Rosa Monckton comments that, 'Speaking as a Roman Catholic, I can say that I saw God in her when she went about what she called her "work" [charity work].'[52] Paul Johnson describes her as 'part Mary Magdalene, part Florence Nightingale...in some ways a lady from the early Christian past, a fun-loving Princess-turned-saint...'[53] Bryan Jobbins, in the article cited earlier, refers to her as a 'secular Madonna.'

But, perhaps, it is Ted Hughes who most clearly draws upon Christian imagery in his poem *6 September 1997*, the last two lines of which poignantly but powerfully make the connection between Diana and the crucifixion:[54]

> Mankind is many rivers
> That only want to run.
> Holy Tragedy and Loss
> Make the many One.
> Mankind is a Holy, crowned
> Mother and her Son.
> For worship, for mourning:
> God is here, is gone.
> Love is broken on the Cross
> The Flower on the Gun.

---

50 Cf William Deedes in MacArthur, p 70: 'She was not a grand person setting out to bestow favours on the poor...Recognizing her own frailty, she was better able to understand and to sympathize with the frailty of others.' See also similar comments by Douglas Hurd in the same volume, p 98.
51 I am grateful to Rev Dr Jeff Astley for sparking off this train of thought.
52 Quoted in MacArthur, p 64.
53 *ibid*, p 151.
54 *ibid*, p 207.

6
Conclusion: The Pastoral Challenge

What can the church learn from the death of Diana and the public reaction to it? Some have criticized the church for an opportunity lost. On this line of reasoning, the events of 31 August–6 September 1997 offered a unique possibility for the proclamation of the gospel that was missed. About this view, three things must be said. Firstly, at the purely logistical level, how might proclamation have been done? The media saturation of those days left no room for any kind of evangelistic message. The policy of editors and managers was to reflect (perhaps shape) the public mood, not to give air time to sermons, lectures or preaching of any kind. Secondly, if the criticism is aimed at the funeral service, then it must be remembered that the service was drawn up by negotiation between Buckingham Palace and Earl Spencer. This left very little freedom of manoeuvre for church authorities who could hardly have refused the wishes of the two. Thirdly, what kind of gospel proclamation do the critics have in mind? To have adopted a hard-edged evangelism would have missed the public mood entirely. Moreover, it would have almost certainly have been open to the charge of emotional manipulation. Just as with any other funeral, what was needed in the aftermath of Diana's death was not evangelistic preaching but pastoral care.

This line of criticism also misses the point that within hours of Diana's death, Christian ministers of all denominations were opening their churches, offering pastoral care to a shocked public and arranging for appropriate means of grieving. This can hardly be described as missing an opportunity.

Nonetheless, there persists a longer-term challenge for the church: how should it respond in times of national spiritual need? The answer is not immediately clear. In a post-Christian, postmodern culture, faith and religion are consigned to the realm of private choice rather than public assent. A national crisis therefore poses particular difficulties since it requires an immediate switch in mind-set. Religion and faith have somehow to be transferred from the private to the public domain, from the interior life-world of the individual to the collective public consciousness.

This is possible while there remains a sufficient reservoir of Christian thought and sentiment within the national psyche. But, as we have seen, the advent of postmodernity has heralded a fragmentation of beliefs such that increasingly the most that can be hoped for is the occasional outward traditional religious observance combined with a pluralism of faith stances. This was precisely the case with Diana's funeral. But, of course, it is light years away from a common religion which would make possible a coherent response in national times of need.

A further challenge can be encapsulated in the following question: what shall we do with Diana as time passes? This is a profoundly pastoral issue. In July 1998 three answers were given. The first was supplied by Earl Spencer: the opening of the Althorp estate for two months each year to allow visitors to view Diana's resting place and to visit a specially-built museum of her life. In so doing, he effectively conceded that there will be continuing interest in making a secular pilgrimage to her 'shrine.' On this model, the pastoral challenge is met by the provision of a quasi-holy place.

The second answer was offered by the Archbishop of York during the course of an interview with *The Sunday Times* newspaper on 5 July 1998 (p 1). Calling into question the pastoral advisability of the Earl's scheme, Dr Hope suggested that it 'was the last thing she would have wanted.' In his view, the country was in danger of 'clinging too much to the icon of Diana' such that there could develop a cult: 'We should be careful that she is not worshipped. That worship should be directed to the God who created her.' Moreover, the nation now needed to let her go so that the grief process could move forward: 'We need to begin to move on, and part of that moving on is the letting go.'

Alongside this, the Archbishop of Canterbury suggested a third answer in *The Times* of 6 July (p 8): the acknowledgment of Diana's death through the use of special prayers of remembrance on Sunday 30 August and the opening of churches around that time for prayer and reflection. We might add: for counselling too. Although the media sought to pit the two archbishops against each other, in reality their strategies are complementary. While York recognizes the dangers of continuing emotional attachment to Diana, Canterbury acknowledges that for the first anniversary, at least, there will need to be provision for pastoral care which acknowledges that people will want some kind of public act. What happens in future years will be interesting to observe.

In conclusion, we need to note that underlying all these answers is yet another pastoral issue: in a postmodern age, how should remembrance of the dead be marked? What rites of passage are appropriate? Within a Christian culture it is possible to address these questions by reference to a shared set of assumptions about life, death, meaning and ultimacy. Common liturgies, acts of worship and religious symbols in this context express a communal memory and attitude. Within a fragmented and pluralistic culture, the task becomes much harder, if not impossible, as shared assumptions cannot be presumed and common acts of worship and symbols become increasingly rare. This is a problem the church needs to face urgently for it will require an institutional culture-shift of massive proportions. As the Diana phenomenon has demonstrated, there is scope for ministry and mission in postmodern societies but on radically different terms from that which has gone before. Unless the church grasps this, it will be condemned to increasing irrelevance.